AF428020

GURU NANAK DEV JI

Compiled by : Bhavneet Kaur

Illustrations : *Generated by* MidJourney

This Book Belongs To

Foreward

DEAR YOUNG READERS,

WELCOME TO THIS SPECIAL BOOK ABOUT GURU NANAK DEV JI, THE FIRST SIKH GURU AND A BELOVED SPIRITUAL TEACHER.

THE ILLUSTRATIONS HAVE BEEN DESIGNED WITH UTMOST CARE, ENSURING THAT THEY ARE VISUALLY APPEALING AND CAPTURE THE ESSENCE OF GURU NANAK DEV JI'S TEACHINGS. EVERY EFFORT HAS BEEN MADE TO PRESENT THE INFORMATION IN A MANNER THAT RESPECTS THE SIKH RELIGION AND ITS BELIEFS, WHILE ALSO MAKING IT ACCESSIBLE AND ENJOYABLE FOR YOUNG READERS LIKE YOU.

THROUGH THE PAGES OF THIS BOOK, YOU WILL LEARN ABOUT THE LIFE, TEACHINGS, AND INCREDIBLE WISDOM OF GURU NANAK DEV JI. YOU WILL DISCOVER THE IMPORTANCE OF LOVE, KINDNESS, AND EQUALITY IN OUR LIVES. THESE VALUES ARE NOT LIMITED TO ANY SPECIFIC RELIGION BUT ARE UNIVERSAL PRINCIPLES THAT WE CAN ALL EMBRACE.

AS YOU READ THIS BOOK, LET YOUR IMAGINATION SOAR AND YOUR HEART BE FILLED WITH JOY

Bhavneet Kaur

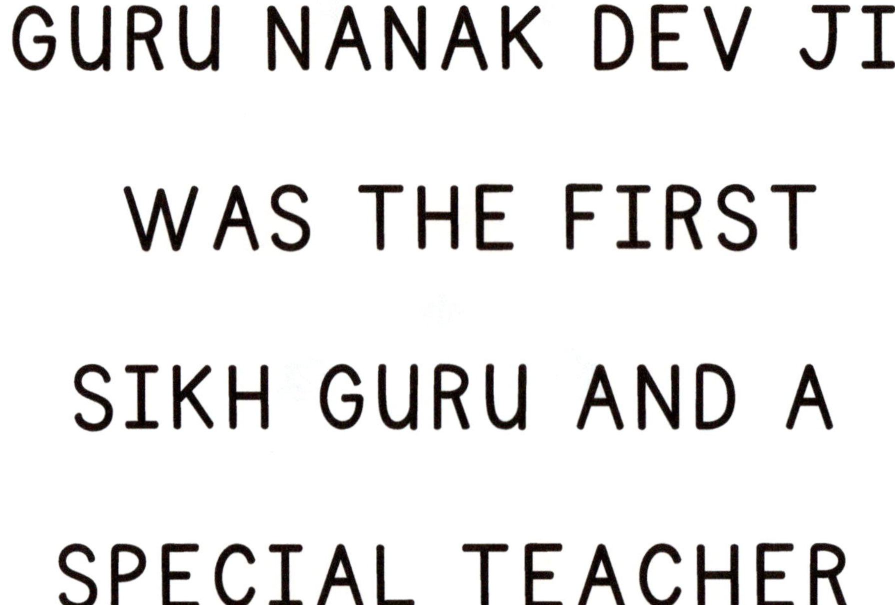

GURU NANAK DEV JI

WAS THE FIRST

SIKH GURU AND A

SPECIAL TEACHER

HE WAS BORN IN THE VILLAGE OF TALWANDI
(NANKANA SAHIB), IN 1469.

GURU NANAK DEV JI'S LOVING FAMILY INCLUDED
HIS PARENTS, MATA TRIPTA JI AND MEHTA KALU
JI, AND SISTER BEBE NANKI

HE HAD A WIFE NAMED MATA SULAKHNI JI.
THEY WERE BLESSED WITH TWO SONS NAMED
SRI CHAND JI AND LAKHMI CHAND JI

HE TAUGHT PEOPLE
TO BE KIND,
HONEST, AND
HELPFUL TO
EVERYONE THEY
MEET

GURU NANAK DEV JI
BELIEVED IN TREATING
EVERYONE EQUALLY &
HAD FOLLOWERS FROM
ALL AROUND

GURU NANAK DEV JI WAS A BRILLIANT POET
AND MUSICIAN.
HE WROTE BEAUTIFUL HYMNS AND MELODIES

GURU NANAK DEV JI'S DEAR COMPANIONS
WERE BHAI MARDANA JI & BHAI BALA JI, WHO
PLAYED THE RABAB AND SANG BEAUTIFUL
MELODIES ALONGSIDE HIM

GURU NANAK DEV JI TRAVELED ON FOUR LONG JOURNEYS CALLED UDASIS, TO DIFFERENT PARTS OF THE WORLD TO SPREAD THE MESSAGE OF PEACE, LOVE, AND UNITY

GURU NANAK DEV JI

WAS KNOWN BY

DIFFERENT NAMES

DURING HIS TRAVELS ON

UDASIS

NANAK LAMA IN TIBET

NANAK FAKIR IN PERSIA

NANAK BHAGAT IN MECCA & MEDINA

NANAK SHAHI IN IRAQ & BAGHDAD

GURU NANAK DEV JI'S

TEACHINGS ARE

WRITTEN IN A HOLY

BOOK CALLED

THE GURU GRANTH

SAHIB

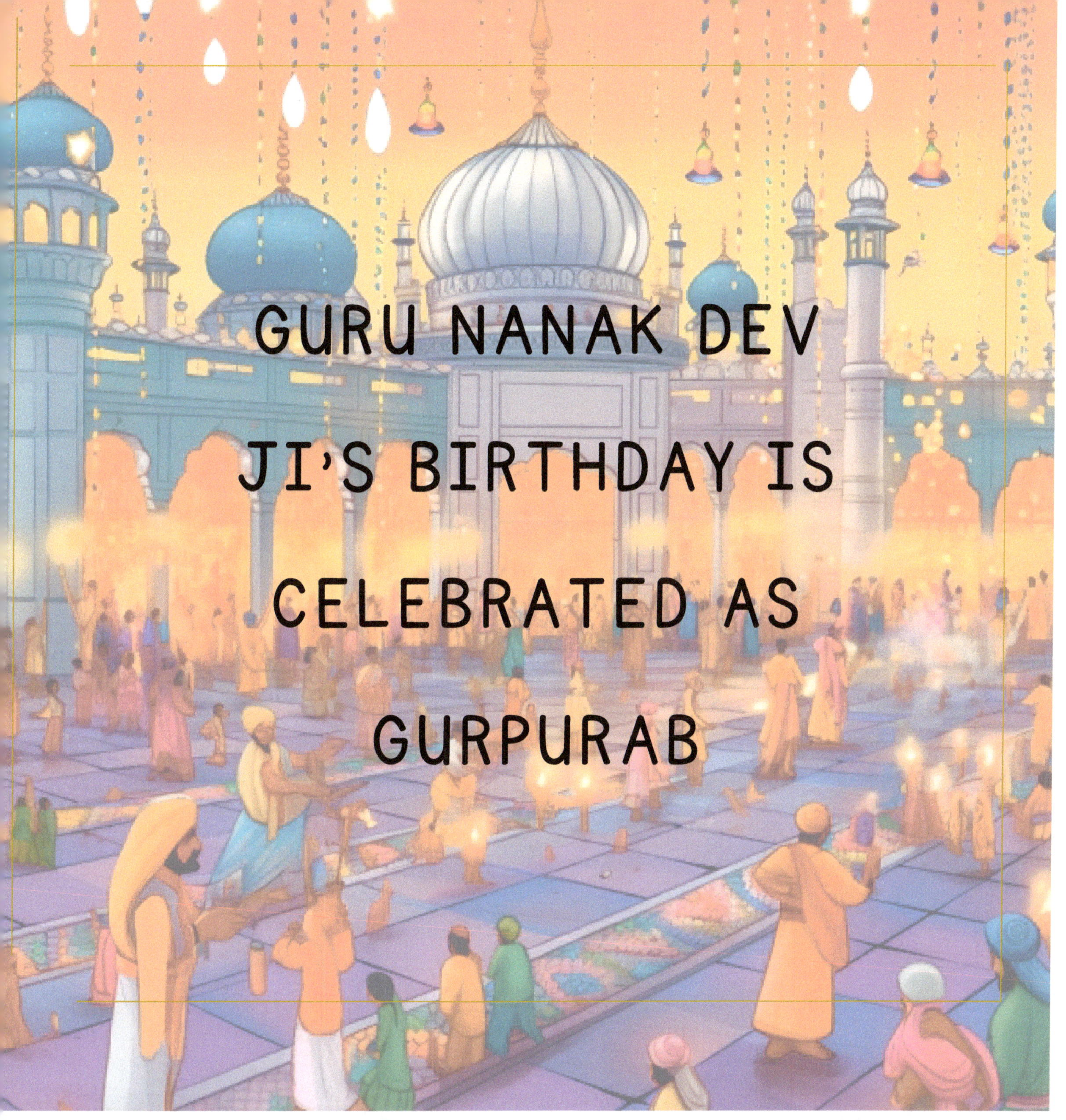
GURU NANAK DEV JI'S BIRTHDAY IS CELEBRATED AS GURPURAB

GURU NANAK DEV JI
BELIEVED THAT EACH
DAY BRINGS LOVE,
NEW THINGS TO
LEARN & HELP OTHERS